PLANTIMAL SAFARI

Plantimals are plants that look like animals. When you go on "safari" through this book, you will see some strange plantimals. Of course, this is not how the plants *really* look — this is how we *imagine* they look.

All of these plants come from the southwestern United States or Mexico except the skunk tree, which is originally from Australia, and the starfish plant from South Africa. The plants all grow in dry, desert regions and have special ways of dealing with the heat. You will find out some of the ways plants cope with the hot desert sun by reading the information given under each plant name.

Enjoy your safari!

Text: Dyan del Gaudio and Kathleen Paul
    Education Department,
    Desert Botanical Garden

Illustrations/Layout: Dyan del Gaudio

Publication of this coloring book was
made possible by a grant from Hal and
Vikkie Bone

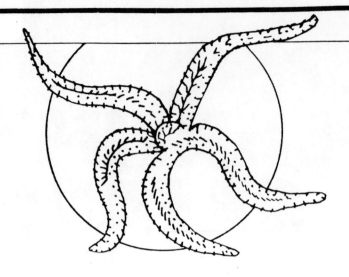

STARFISH PLANT

The flower of this plant looks like a starfish and can grow as big as twelve inches wide. The starfish plant is a succulent. Succulents are plants that can store water in their stems, leaves or roots. This stored water keeps the plants from getting thirsty during months when no rain falls.

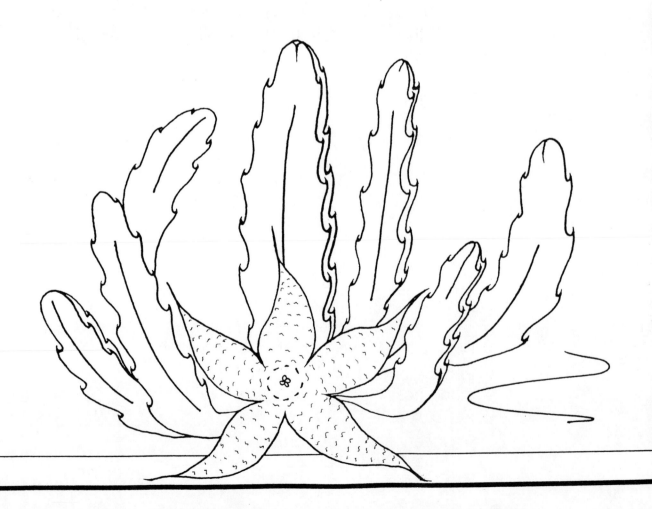

TEDDY BEAR CHOLLA

The teddy bear cholla is a cactus that may look soft and cuddly like a teddy bear, but watch out for those spines! If you brush up against them, a section of the plant might break off and stick to you. A new plant can grow from this section when it falls to the ground.

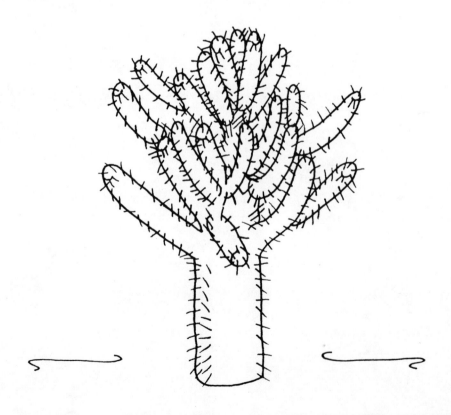

BUNNY EARS PRICKLY PEAR

It is easy to see why this plant is called bunny ears. The sections that look like the ears of a rabbit are actually called pads. These pads store water which helps the plant survive in the dry desert.

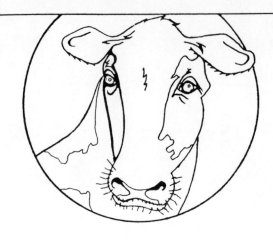

COW TONGUE PRICKLY PEAR

This is another kind of prickly pear. It has pads that are the same shape as a cow's tongue. Like other cactus, a waxy outer coating helps seal in water. No matter how hot and dry the weather is, the pads stay nice and moist inside.

GRIZZLY BEAR PRICKLY PEAR

The spines on this prickly pear sure look "grizzly" — just like the fur of a grizzly bear. The spines help shade the plant from the hot desert sun. Each pad is fully covered with these long spines, so this should be one cool cactus.

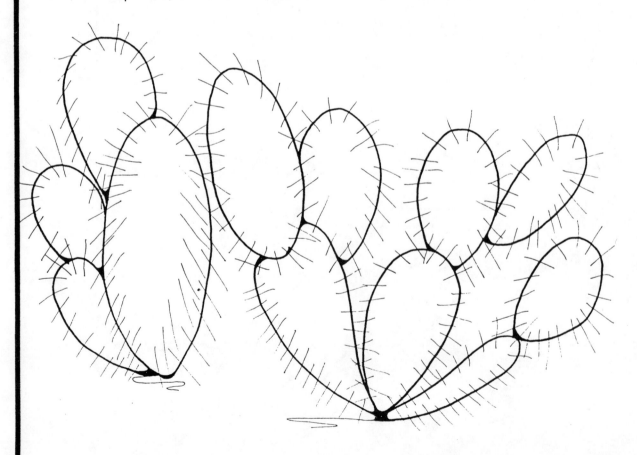

BEAVERTAIL PRICKLY PEAR

The pads of this prickly pear are shaped like a beaver's tail. The dots on the pads are called glochids. All prickly pears have these tiny, hairlike spines. These spines can really get under your skin — be careful not to touch!

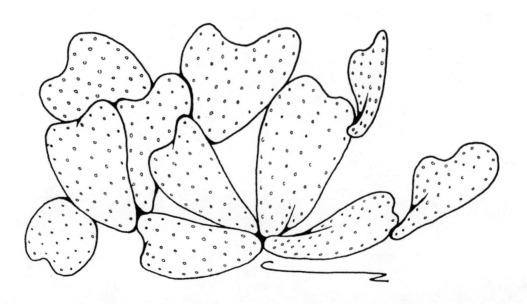

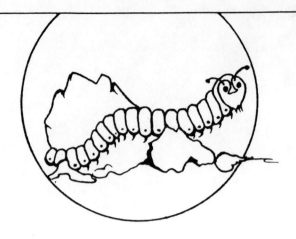

CATERPILLAR CACTUS

This plant creeps along the ground and looks like a big, fat caterpillar. Its spines are tough enough to poke through leather. You will often see many of them growing in one place.

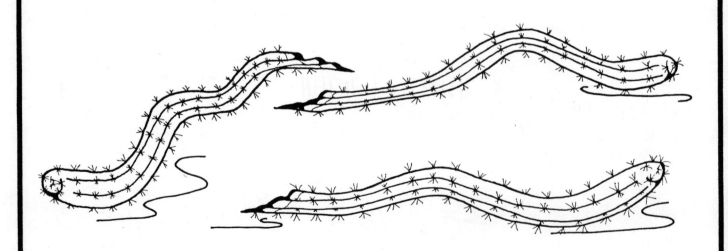

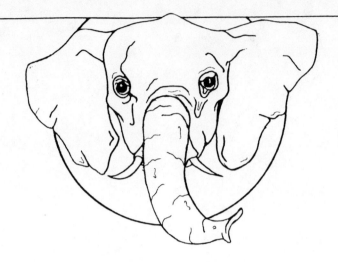

ELEPHANT CACTUS

This cactus got its name because the bottom part looks as if an elephant's foot is growing out of the ground. A full grown plant can be more than 50 feet tall and can weigh even more than a real elephant.

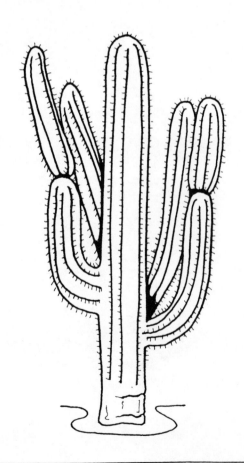

HEDGEHOG CACTUS

A hedgehog is a small animal covered with stiff hairs or spines that it uses to protect itself from other animals. The spines of this cactus look like the stiff hairs of the hedgehog. Sometimes these spines protect the cactus from hungry animals who might like to eat it.

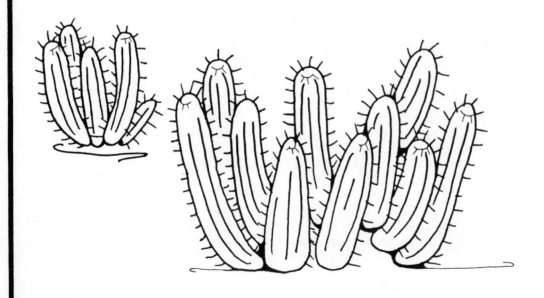

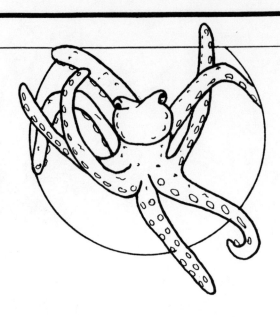

OCTOPUS CACTUS

The arms of this cactus bend like the tentacles of an octopus swimming in the sea. The arm is really the plant stem. When one of the stems touches the ground, it can take root and grow into a new plant.

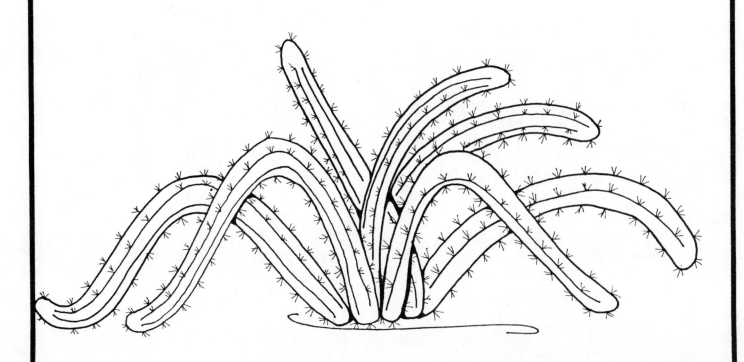

CAT CLAW TREE

The thorns on this tree are shaped like the claws of a cat. They are very sharp and can hook into your clothes if you get too close. If you have ever been scratched by a cat, you will know why you should be careful when you walk by this tree.

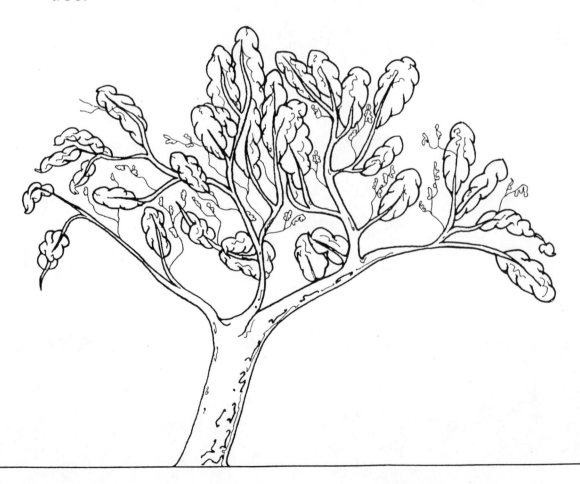

SKUNK TREE

The plants you have seen so far all look something like the animal they were named after. This tree doesn't look like a skunk, but if you get close enough you will notice a strange odor. Close your eyes, take a sniff and ... you guessed it! It smells just like a skunk.

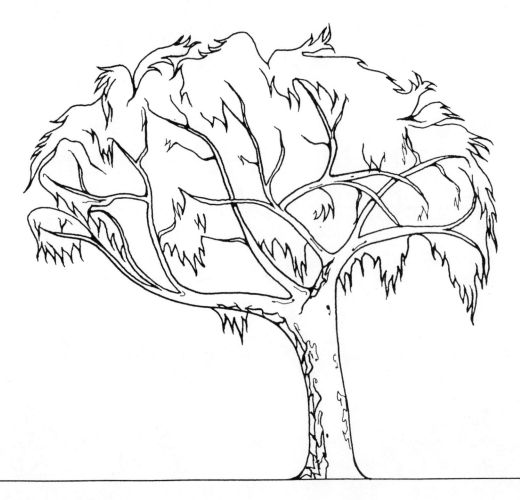

Have you ever seen a plant that looks like an animal? Look around and I bet you can find a tree, flower or some other plant that reminds you of a certain animal. In these spaces, create your own plantimals.

PLANT LIST

Scientists around the world all use the same name when talking about a certain plant. This is known as a plant's *botanical name.* People from different areas sometimes make up their own names for plants. These names are called common names.

Listed below are the common names and *botanical names* of the plants used in this book.

Common Name	Botanical Name
Starfish Plant	*Stapelia gigantea*
Teddy Bear Cholla	*Opuntia bigelovii*
Bunny Ears Prickly Pear	*Opuntia microdasys*
Cow Tongue Prickly Pear	*Opuntia lindheimeri var. linguiformis*
Grizzly Bear Prickly Pear	*Opuntia erinacea*
Beavertail Prickly Pear	*Opuntia basilaris*
Caterpillar Cactus	*Stenocereus eruca*
Elephant Cactus	*Pachycereus pringlei*
Hedgehog Cactus	*Echinocereus engelmannii*
Octopus Cactus	*Stenocereus alamosensis*
Cat Claw Tree	*Acacia greggii*
Skunk Tree	*Acacia rostellifera*